Mind Control Techniques

The Secrets of Manipulation, Deception, Hypnosis, Persuasion and Human Psychology

By Ken Talley

I0437776

Table of Contents

Introduction

When you hear the term 'mind control,' what do you think about? What does it mean to you?

Perhaps you're like so many people out there who conjure up thoughts of nefarious people making others do their evil bidding. That's the stuff of poor Hollywood movies and bad fiction.

Mind control isn't about taking over someone's thoughts, controlling their actions, and making them do whatever you wanted them to do. Sure, there are a number of people out there who can do those sorts of things, but they're usually called cults, or cult leaders.

No, mind control in the sense that we're going to focus on in this book has to do with *influence*.

There are many ways that a person can influence someone to change their opinion, alter their perspective, and get them to agree with them, or get them to do something for them. Okay, so that sounds similar to what I just described earlier, doesn't it?

Well, let's set that aside for the moment. You can use mind control to make people do things for you.

Charles Manson did it.

David Koresh did it down in Waco, Texas.

Countless politicians have done it to win office.

But mind control can help you influence others, to get the things you want, to convince them that your ideas, your perspective, or your point of view is right.

You don't need to be an evil, mad scientist to have mind control work for you. You don't need to be a corrupt politician, either.

In this book, I'm going to outline some of the key aspects to mind control and show you how they work and what you can do to improve your life, get the job you dream of, have the ideal relationship, and even save a ton of money on your next car, house, or major purchase.

It's all well within your reach, so let's take a ride and see what is out there waiting for you.

Chapter 1: The Basics of Mind Control

Let's take a quick trip back in time for a moment, shall we? All the way back to when you were a wee little lass.

There was a toy that you just *had to have*. Your best friend didn't have it yet. No other kids in school had this toy. Yet.

You absolutely had to have it, didn't you? You saw it on the store shelf and you knew right then and there that this was your mission in life. This was your *purpose*, to get that toy.

So what did you do?

Did you ask your mother? Did you go to your dad after she said no and tell him that 'Mom told me to ask you'?

What happened when they said no? What did you do next when they told you that you could ask for it for your birthday or Christmas? You thought, but that's *forever* away.

There was *no way* you would stand for that. You had to have that toy **now**, before anyone else had it.

So you probably went into one or two paths. You might have moved onto the old puppy dog eyes, the sad pouty lips, and the fake tears that you had learned to conjure up at will. You stood around near your mother or father trying to get them to pay attention to you, to that hard work that you were putting into that sad, devastated expression.

After all, it had worked to get you the candy bar at the store the other day. Why wouldn't it work now? You're not thinking that the candy bar was a buck and the toy is $200. Money doesn't mean anything to you yet … you're too young.

But that strategy didn't work out and you were told to go away, to leave them alone. Manipulating their emotions didn't work. They didn't feel sorry for you.

So next you turned to storming off, throwing a temper tantrum, and you were determined to keep this going until they gave in. Grounding, punishment, all of that be damned, you *were going to win this war!*

You got grounded for a week. You gave up that poor persuasive technique.

So now you turned to your old pal *deception*. If you could tell your parents that you need money for a school project, or a trip, you could go and get that toy yourself. As long as you have it, you could deal with any repercussions they throw your way.

But that didn't work either.

Well, at least you tried, right? You tried the three main facets of mind control: manipulation, deception, and persuasion.

You just weren't very good at it.

Now you're older and ready to take it to a whole new level. You're not interested in getting a toy, though. You're interested in getting a date with the hot gym trainer who never has a ring on.

You're interested in landing the best job of your life.

You're interested in convincing your neighbor to sell you his three year old power boat for less than market value.

Everywhere you turn you see opportunities to build your life up from the ashes, from the ground up, and so far, to this point in time, you feel like you're doing nothing but waiting in line while others just seem to get around the line and get on the ride first.

It's not fair, but then again ... no one ever said that life would be fair.

What is Mind Control?

At its core, mind control is nothing more than the ability to *convince someone that you are right.*

Sounds simple enough, right?

It's not some dark art form. It's not a nefarious activity. It could be. Depending on how you use it, you might be considered a genius or an evil entity.

A knife sits on the counter … it doesn't do anything bad, right? You use that knife to cut up tomatoes and carrots and make a full salad. It wasn't evil.

Of course, some people would use it to stab someone, to cause harm, to kill. That makes the person using it for that person evil or bad or mean.

The knife is still a tool.

That's what mind control is: just a tool.

How you use it will be entirely up to you. It's not illegal, although there are going to be limitations to what you can do with it. If you are deceptive and steal money from someone pretending you represent a charity, then you're committing a crime.

I'm not going to teach you any of that here. If you're trying to find the keys to those types of mind control tricks, those *con jobs*, then look elsewhere.

What I'm going to teach you is how you use what you have, how you can shape your words and your message to get what you want.

It's not easy. Mind control is one of the toughest skills to learn, but once you have the ability to change someone's mind, then you have the ability to do anything you want in this life, and that's not something many of us can actually say.

Why You Need to Learn Mind Control

Everywhere you turn, people are trying to control you. Most of the time you don't even notice it. That's because they are skilled at mind control.

The ads that you see on the TV screen, the Big Mac or Whopper that fills all 50-inches of that flat screen TV are designed to influence your mind. Those are deceptive images. They are painted burgers, fake patties, fake lettuce, and glazed buns, all done to make the burger look mouth watering.

And when your mouth does water, your mind has been effectively controlled.

When you learn about mind control, you'll not only empower yourself to be more effective at controlling others, but you'll be on the constant lookout for how others are trying to manipulate you.

There are three key mind control techniques that I'll talk about in this book: manipulation, deception, and persuasion.

There's another, too, but that's reserved for professionals. It's called hypnosis and we'll touch on it briefly in the next chapter.

Chapter 2: Different Types of Mind Control

As I've mentioned already, you have your three basic types of mind control.

Manipulation.

Deception.

Persuasion.

You also have one that is used by psychoanalysts and certain counselors, as well as some parlor trick magicians, and that's called Hypnosis.

We'll start off with the ones that we should be learning.

Manipulation

When you try to convince someone to do something for you because otherwise you could become injured, for example, even though there's not much risk, then you're manipulating them.

Manipulation is one of the first mind control techniques that we learn in life.

The kid who wants the candy bar at the store, whose mother says no, and then who starts to cry, then wail, and throw stuff is manipulating his mother to get what he wants.

He is basically telling her, 'I will stop my bad behavior and keep from embarrassing you further if you just give in and get me what I want.'

It's manipulation in its rarest and rawest form.

But it can be highly effective.

Even adults use this raw form of manipulation all the time. The temper tantrum, or the threatening harm upon the girlfriend if she were to leave him … those are forms of manipulation.

That's not something you want to be a part of. It doesn't make you a stronger person and doesn't get you what you want for long.

But there are many other forms of manipulation that you could use. To manipulate someone means that you are trying to force them to see your point of view, or to give you what you want, without having to highlight the benefits that it could offer them to do so.

Many ads that you'll find online that promise you some great results for your life, whether it's to lose weight or get the girl you want, that tell you that you *must act now*, that *supplies are limited* or *this deal won't last* are all manipulating you.

They're not deceiving you, unless those claims are false. Assuming they are true, they are manipulating you, giving you limited amount of time to make your decision.

When people are put up against a wall when it comes to making a decision, they are more susceptible to other forms of persuasion and mind control.

Think about this situation: you go to shop for a used car. You see something you like, you know the Blue Book value on it, but the salesperson isn't willing to negotiate too much with you.

You give him your final low price and then stand up to leave. You've taken control of the negotiation away from him. You're manipulating him into action. Now, he's either going to call you back to 'go talk to the boss' or he's going to let you leave. Assuming your offer is fair, then he'll be calling you back in.

You've just played the game with him. You *manipulated* him into action. He thought you were going to walk away, he *knew* that your offer was fair, but he was assuming that you'd give in. He was trying to manipulate or deceive you, but you won that mind control game.

But how many of us actually play the game properly? Not many. That's why used car dealers and salesmen make a lot of money, a lot more than they would if people have better information about these mind control techniques.

You see, though? It is mind control, but it's not evil. It's just learning to play the game to get what you want and win.

Think about this way, if you need: Tiger Woods was the best golfer in the world for 10 years. No one could take him down. Until 2009, if he had a lead going into the final round, or even if he were tied, he won almost every single time.

He intimidated his opponents with his focus, his power, and his mind. He *manipulated* them into second guessing themselves on every shot when it mattered most. Half the time they fell apart. He didn't need to beat them; he already did.

Deception

Okay, so now we get to the most common form of mind control: deception.

What is deception? It's the absence or alteration of truth to try and get something that you want. In other words, it's the lie.

It could be a small white lie to avoid getting in trouble or it could be a much bigger lie to win a prize, election, or ace a test.

When you use deception as a form of mind control, you need to be very careful. People can get hurt as a result of deception. If you don't worry about those things, if you don't care *who* gets hurt as a result of your deception, then you're going to find that problems follow you everywhere you go throughout your entire life and at some point in time, you're going to turn around, look at the people whom you've surrounded yourself with, and question whether any of them actually like you for you, if any of them are honest with you.

However, deception can be a powerful tool in the art of mind control.

I mentioned one good example with the advertisements. How about clothing fashions. You have models that are skin and bones and we're deceived into thinking that's actually attractive. If you want those outfits to look as good on you as they do on those models, then you need to lose weight, exercise, or something.

Yet you want those fashions *because* they look so good on other people. You're deceived into believing that they could make you look as hot as those models.

If you think that's stupid, then ask yourself why so many companies spend so much money on advertising. That's because deception works.

You never wear a suit and tie, but you did on that last job interview. Why? *Because you wanted the employer to **think** that you're more professional looking than you normally are.*

You tried to *deceive* him or her.

Nothing wrong with it, though. You just need to know and keep your limitations intact.

Persuasion

The most powerful form of mind control is persuasion. It's also the toughest. I won't lie or deceive you on that.

When you want to change someone's mind and get them to agree with you, then you need to *persuade* them. You need to show them why changing their mind would benefit them.

Everywhere you turn today, there are people trying to persuade others to change their opinions, usually with regard to politics. The nation is more divided now than at any other time in modern history, but no one's really listening to facts; they're allowing themselves to be manipulated by words, by labels, and by ideologies. Then they revert to name calling and at that point, all hope of persuading someone to change their mind is lost.

Persuasion is amazing, but it requires a solid grasp on facts, on language, presentation, tone of voice, and so much more.

However, once you persuade someone to change their mind, it's going to be that much tougher for someone else to change it back.

Hypnosis

Hypnosis, as noted, is used primarily by mental healthcare professionals and some gypsy magicians. Real hypnosis is a process by which you relax a person and their mind to the point where they can actively access the subconscious part of their brain.

You can cause a lot of emotional harm to a person by trying to hypnotize them. It's not worth it, you won't get someone to quack like a duck or do other parlor tricks, and you wouldn't get them to look the other way if you want them to.

Hypnosis, as a form of mind control, is about healing. So don't bother trying to get involved in it. Leave that to the professionals.

So now that we know the different forms of mind control, it's time that we began working on each of them. The best, most skilled people at mind control are those who are able to rely on two or all three of these forms of mind control.

The more tools that you have in your control, the easier it will be for you to get the things that you want.

Chapter 3: Mastering Manipulation

When you want to manipulate someone, you want to force them to change their opinion, their mind, or do what *you* want them to do without having to persuade them.

You need to understand their motivations, and your own, in order to successfully manipulate them. You need to be willing to step up and take charge of a conversation or situation.

It takes a lot of time, patience, and practice to learn the proper art of manipulation.

Of course, the word 'manipulate' has a negative connotation to it. You might be thinking about it in terms of making someone do something that they just don't want to do.

Yet, consider this: if someone does something, even though they 'claim' that they don't want to, there is enough desire to want to do it ... they just need the proper conviction.

Or manipulation.

After all, you're not going to get that used car for $5,000 when the dealer paid $5,000 for it, *unless the dealer just wants to get rid of it*. If the car is sitting on the lot for a year, the dealership is losing money on it. So, if you know how to manipulate the situation and manage to get it for that price, it's not that you forced them to sell ... it's that you took the choice away from them, for the most part.

We hear too often about how people claim they were manipulated into voting for one candidate, or law, or something, even though they didn't really want to.

Seriously?

No one is forced to vote for anything. They may buy into the lies and the false promises, but if they don't do their homework, if they don't look into the facts about the candidate or the bill or whatever, then that's their fault.

They *made themselves that much easier to manipulate*.

Okay, so now that you know manipulation isn't an evil act, how do you make it work?

Keys to Making it Work

First, you need to *know the person*.

You need to know the person you are trying to manipulate. You need to understand their tendencies, their motivations, and the way they think about certain things.

If you don't know anything about the person you want to manipulate, then good luck succeeding with it.

You may be thinking that since you're going into an interview for a job, there's no possible way that you could know anything about the person interviewing you. Maybe not, especially if you don't even know their name.

But you can learn about the business, about the company.

What are they looking for? What are their long-term goals? What is their idea of the ideal employee?

Maybe that suit and tie isn't what they're looking for. Maybe they want someone who is comfortable with themselves and not trying to impress with dress.

What about that girl that you have a crush on? Learn about her (don't stalk her, dig through her trash, or anything creepy or illegal like that). Talk to her. Don't ask her out, but talk. Get to know her. If she's at a bar, sit near her and listen to some of her conversations.

You can learn a lot about people by catching their personal conversations with friends. We tend to let our guard down when among friends more than at any other time in our life.

What about the aforementioned car dealer? You really want that car you've been eyeing for a while. Who in the company makes the most deals? Who is more desperate for a sale?

Do you have common interests?

Do you have anything common in your background?

Do you like the same sports team? Maybe the salesperson or the girl you like loves the Red Sox but you're a die hard Yankees fan. There's no reason you can't throw on a Red Sox cap for a minute. It won't kill you.

What are you willing to do in order to manipulate them?

Next, you need to *master communication.*

The moment that a person begins to control the conversation is the moment they are the manipulators.

If you sit there and let your mark (the person you're trying to manipulate) control the conversation and ask all sorts of questions of you, then you're not going to be influencing them in any way, shape, or form.

Too many of us are passive when it comes to relationships and interactions.

The salesperson *controls* the conversation the moment he or she asks what you're interested in. Ever notice how they lead you to the product they *think* you'll like?

They don't really care what you want. They are trying to manipulate *you* to help close the sale.

Being articulate is a powerful way to control conversations. Being able to state your position in few words is powerful.

When asked a question, redirect it back to them. Get them to talk about themselves, rather than having to talk about you.

Deep down, most of us *love* having people who *listen* to us. It makes us feel special, as though we really matter.

Turn the conversation around and control it. Like this:

Love interest: So, where did you go to school?

You: Briddle High. What about you?

Love interest: Oh, I went to Carmel.

You (right away): You know, I've heard of Carmel, but I've never been there. Tell me what it's like.

In this example, the manipulator now controls the conversation. He answered the question, then redirected it, *then*, he didn't ask another one, but demanded her to tell him more about that place.

When you control the language and the tone of a conversation, people will answer without even thinking about it. They will become drawn into the conversation and even though they're talking about themselves, it doesn't quite feel one-sided.

This control of the conversation moves you to the closing.

Ask her out.

You: Where can I pick you up tomorrow night for dinner?

You' didn't ask her out. You just moved in with confidence, having already won her over by manipulating the conversation, by controlling it.

Finally, learn to *read body language*.

Is the person leaning in? Are they engaged? Or are they guarded? Seek out the topics that loosen them up and make them more willing to be manipulated.

You could read tons of books on body language. But, for an example, a person with their arms crossed over their chest is 'closed' to what you're saying.

Someone who leans in, who makes strong eye contact, is engaged, willing.

The Pitfalls

Manipulation will not work against someone who is guarded against it. It will only work on people who *want* to be manipulated, either on a conscious or subconscious level.

The good thing is that most people want to be manipulated.

When you're manipulated, you don't need to really think for yourself. You don't need to have to make decisions.

That's a big deal to most people, even though you may not realize it.

However, you'll quickly develop a keen eye for those who are on guard against being manipulated.

When you read closed body language or other cues that they are not interested, you need to know when to back off, regroup, and shift gears. Just because they are guarded doesn't mean you can't control their mind.

The Limitations

As noted earlier, the key limitation with manipulation is that the person must be willingly engaged in the manipulation. If they aren't, then you're forcing them against their will and that's not likely to happen through open, honest manipulation.

For example, you could kidnap a person's precious cat and tell them to steal money from their job, but that's a crime. That's not manipulation for mind control. That's manipulation through force.

Don't confuse the two.

Manipulation for mind control is a process by which you achieve results without physical coercion, threatening harm, or other criminal behaviors.

Chapter 4: Perfecting Persuasion

I'm not going to lie and say that persuasion is easy.

It's not. It's *hard*.

It takes a lot of time and practice to master. Once you do master it, though, you're going to find that there are so many new doors that open to you.

Persuasion shares something in common with manipulation and that is you *must know the person you're trying to persuade.*

Those who are closed off to new ideas or certain things are going to be far more challenging than those who are followers, who actively seek out those who can take charge.

Observe the person you want to persuade and determine whether they are closed off or whether they are an open book (or a blank slate, so to speak).

Just because someone is closed off doesn't mean that they won't be persuaded. It will take more time and effort on your part to be successful with the persuasion. The keys will be the same, but the amount of time that you have to invest in that person will increase.

Mastering Articulation

Persuasion is about articulating your idea and backing it up with *facts*. It's those pesky facts that get to some people.

If you come up against a person who isn't willing to 'see' facts for what they are, but will continue to be rigid in their point of view, then they are *very* closed to new ideas.

When you begin the process of persuading someone, you need to have your logic and points in clear order.

What do you want to communicate to the target?

What points do you want to make clear?

What is his/her starting point? What are their thoughts on this already?

Gather as many supporting facts as you can. Express them simply and clearly. Don't try to be fancy and use big words when a few, short ones would suffice. Don't try to sound smarter than you are. Don't try to sound like someone who has been in the industry for 20 years if you only have limited exposure or experience.

Be genuine.

Whatever you do, in order to be articulate on a subject, you need to be *practiced* with it. You need to be able to speak openly and comfortably about the topic. If you can't, then you're going to ramble. You're going to go off on tangents when talking, worried that you're not getting the point across.

Practice your talking points in front of a mirror first. Get comfortable with what you're trying to say. Sure, it may feel weird doing that, but most great orators or speakers begin by practicing in front of a mirror.

Once you become more comfortable with your talking points, ask a close, trusted friend for help. Practice with them. Have them act as your target, with the same type of questions they might ask, or with the same cynicism or doubt.

When you practice these talking points, you improve your articulation, and that is the fundamental key to being successful with persuasion.

A person who is articulate, who knows the facts, who has data that he or she can point to in order to support their facts, the person who is *confident* in what they are talking about, will have a great chance of persuading someone to change their mind, or give permission, or to give you what you're looking for with this interaction.

If you are a lazy talker, meaning you tend to slur your words, mumble, or talk too softly, you're going to cause the target to strain to hear what you're saying. Anytime that someone has to work too hard to hear someone, they're spending too much energy and effort on the listening that they're not paying attention to the message.

The more articulate and clear you are, the stronger your persuasion tactics will be.

Limitations

The limitations of persuasion are in two things: the openness of the target individual and the facts that you've chosen to support your claims.

First, if the target has their 'mind made up,' that doesn't mean you won't be able to change it with the right persuasion. It just means it's going to be much tougher to break down their walls and get the facts past their gates.

If you support your claims with facts that are weak, come from biased sources, or cause your target to immediately shell up, then you lose right away.

For example, if you're trying to convince your liberal minded friend that it's the Senate's fault for something and not the conservative led House, citing Fox News as your source will not help your cause any. However, if you had found a source from a left leaning 'news' source, like the New York Times, that supported your claim, then you will be better equipped to make an impact.

It's the same as if you were talking to a professor and trying to convince him or her that your thesis on vaccinations is a quality topic, that you can prove common understanding to be wrong, and then you base your assumptions on Wikipedia, you've already lost him or her (Wikipedia is considered the bane of college research papers due to the poor citation and numerous incorrect information usually posted on the pages).

Choose facts that are neutrally based. Avoid propaganda as your support system. The more powerful the source of information, the more powerful your argument will become.

So what if we're talking about you trying to persuade a salesperson to sell you the item you want at the price you're offering?

You should have plenty of sources that highlight how much the car is worth in the condition it's in, and have a mechanic check the vehicle out for you. They could tell you it's in excellent condition, but the mechanic you hired to look it over says that there are some issues with the exhaust, the brakes will need replacing in about 5,000 miles or so, and there are some interior issues that you might not have thought about.

That gives you leverage. Once you can persuade the seller that your price is fair, he'll either agree or decide to wait for the next sucker. If the car has been sitting on the lot for a long time, the more you do to persuade him, the more likely you'll be to get the car for the money you're offering.

Just keep in mind, though, that if the person is closed off to your ideas, they aren't listening to facts. They don't care. You could have a person who believes that the rain is acidic and refuses to step foot outside in it and nothing you say or do will convince them otherwise.

If you can read your target, and you know that they are open about potentially changing their mind, then you'll be in a better position to persuade them to agree with what you want.

Things to Consider

Persuading someone to do what you want takes time. If you're looking for a quick solution, the smaller the leap of faith a person would have to take, the easier and quicker it will be for them to agree to what you want.

The bigger the leap, the more reluctant they will be to accept that challenge.

If you're 17 and trying to convince your mother and father to let you go away for the weekend with friends for your end of school celebration, that's probably a major hurdle for most parents.

First, you want to assuage their fears. What would be their primary concerns? That you'll do drugs, drink, or have sex while you're away from home. If you're planning an honest, wholesome fun time away with friends, tell them that. Find ways to convince them that you're not going to be putting yourself in harm's way.

Next, speak to reality. You're going away to college in about two or three months. They won't have a say any longer on what you do, so they should learn to let go and trust you now.

Tell them exactly where you'll be, who you'll be with, and don't lie, otherwise that's deception, not persuasion. Let them know what you'll be doing. Once you give them the facts, it will be easier for them to take that leap of faith.

If you have a history of lying to this person, though, you may have to rely on other mind control tactics, such as deception or manipulation.

Persuasion is the purest form of mind control and though it's also the toughest to master, when you do, it will be well worth the effort.

Chapter 5: Doctoring Deception

Deception is a tricky subject to talk about. When we hear the word 'deception,' we really tend to think of something that is nefarious and almost evil.

The truth of the matter is that almost all of us lie, and on a regular basis. For some, lying is just a part of life. They do it as easily and without forethought as they do anything else. For others, lying is not as easy as some make it seem.

Look to our political leaders and you will see, for most of them, deception is part and parcel for their jobs. They will tell their constituents what they want to hear to get elected, and they will lie to their colleagues to get what they want.

They can easily stand in front of a television camera and lie to the people and then turn away and not feel any remorse for it.

Deception is not easy for someone who has a guilty conscience. If you feel bad about what you're doing, or you don't think that what you've done is fair, or right, then it's going to weigh more heavily on your mind when you actually deceive someone.

Is it Right for You?

So, the question then becomes 'is deception as a mind control technique right for you?'

The truth is that only you can answer that question. You need to resolve that within your own mind and your own heart. If you're going to lose sleep over the deception, then it's not going to be right for you.

We could be talking about you lying to get the job you've always wanted. That might be one means to an end, but what if you keep moving up the corporate ladder; would you still be okay with the deception? Many people will say that the ends justify the means, but that depends on the means.

If you had to flatten the tires on your neighbor's car so that you could get to the store before him and get that last roast for Thanksgiving dinner, would you be okay with that? While that's borderline criminal, it's still a deceptive scheme.

Let's talk about drugs and sports. From Lance Armstrong to Barry Bonds, from Alex Rodriguez to Mark McGuire, drugs have been a part of professional sports for a long time. Performance enhancing drugs are designed to help an athlete get an advantage over his competitors.

Is it fair? Absolutely not. Many sports ban most supplements, but science is always trying to find a way to bend the rules, or at least get around them for a time being.

Do you think any of those guys who get caught using performance enhancing drugs really feel bad when they're caught?

Not likely. They weren't in it to set records because they believed they were the best; they were looking for an edge because they *knew* they couldn't do it otherwise. Barry Bonds *knew* he would forever be lost in the annals of baseball history unless he stepped up and did whatever was necessary to leave his mark.

He denies his use, even though all of the circumstantial evidence states otherwise. There are aspects that *every single human body* follows as it ages, yet Barry's body went against nature and got much bigger as he approached 40.

Alex Rodriguez continues to deny the allegations that he used performance enhancing drugs. His career is basically over now, serving an entire year long suspension at 39, but he shows no remorse.

Lance Armstrong repeatedly denied doping during his 7 Tour de France cycling championships and now that he's finally admitted it, being stripped of those titles, he claims that 'everyone is doping.'

For these guys, they just don't see how their cheating hurts anyone, and even though they deny it, even when caught, they don't lose sleep over it.

Will cheating or deceiving someone get you what you want? Maybe. But you have to live with the repercussions. If you can do that, then that's on you.

How to Deceive

Deception is an art of lying, essentially. When you deceive someone, you're telling them one thing, but doing or planning something completely different.

"Mom, can I use the car?"

"What for honey?"

"I'm going to pick up Robbie from work, bring him home."

"Okay. How long will you be?"

"I don't know. We might go hang out at the arcade later."

"Okay. Don't be late."

"I won't."

You had no intention of picking up Robbie. You're going to see your girlfriend at her house because her parents are away.

That was deception. Now, if you don't get caught, it was successful.

But you see how deception works. You deceive someone by telling them something that you're sure (or quite sure) that they will agree to. As a kid, you had a pretty good idea about who your parents liked of your friends, who they thought was trustworthy, and who they wouldn't have a problem with you hanging out.

In this example, the mother obviously doesn't trust this girl that her son's dating. Maybe there's a good reason for that lack of trust. The kid deceives his mother by focusing her attention on his friend, someone she knows, likes, and trusts.

When you want to deceive someone, you need to know what they will agree to, and you need to be able to back up that deception, if needed.

Think about asking someone out on a date. You decide that you've had enough of going to bars to try and meet someone. So you build an online profile. You don't flat out lie, but you stretch the truth. Maybe you're 5'10" and state that you're six feet tall. Maybe you have a belly but state that you're 'athletic.'

You find some pictures of you from ten years ago and post those. You might be working at the mall but list your occupation as a professional corporate supervisor.

All of those things are deceptive. The farther away from truth and reality you go with your deception, the harder it's going to be to maintain the façade for long. Once a crack forms, the whole thing could come tumbling down.

Let's say you meet a woman online and email back and forth for a long time before meeting. Now she wants to meet, but you know that she's going to realize that those pictures are old. Now what? You could deceive her some more and delay the actual face to face meeting, or you could be honest with her.

She might expect something like that.

But what if she's thinking the pictures of the house you've listed as 'your home' is actually your parents' home and you're still living with them?

As you can see, good deception requires *planning*. That means you need to think well into the future and cover your bases.

Abraham Lincoln once noted that an honest man doesn't need a good memory.

But liars and deceivers do. If you can't keep your deception going, eventually it will catch up with you. That could lead to you losing your job, losing your relationship, and even more.

Some deceptions could land you in jail, depending on how offended the person you deceived becomes.

Why We Deceive

The question is an important one to consider. We deceive because it's easier to get what we want sooner, rather than later.

We deceive because we don't think that we will be able to get what we want without it.

We deceive because we have become a society bent on immediate gratification.

It has become almost culturally accepted and even expected that people will lie to get what they want.

The men and women who dress up for interviews, when they never wear suits or power dresses normally. That's deception.

The average relationship fails after the first year. Why? Because during that first year, each person is trying to impress their partner by acting or being something different than they really are at heart. In other words, they are deceiving their partner. That usually ends after the first year, and that's when those relationships fall apart.

We are taught early on in life to lie. Our parents and culture tell us a host of lies when we're kids. Santa Claus, the Tooth Fairy, and so on are lies told to help keep children comfortable, or to get them to listen.

So we learn how to deceive early on; it becomes part of our programming.

Is Deception Wrong?

As noted earlier, it's entirely up to you to determine whether deception is right or wrong. If you feel that the ends justify the means, if you don't believe anyone will actually be hurt by your deception, then you're likely going to see it as an effective mind control tool.

However, the more adept you become at deception, the more power you will gain as a result. With that increased power comes

increased risk and responsibility.

Let's talk about that next.

Chapter 6: With Great Power Comes Great Responsibility

When we begin to develop your mind control techniques, you're going to discover that you have an incredible amount of new found power. You will have the ability to completely alter other people's opinions, their mind, and decisions.

You will be able to get just about anything you want.

And that kind of power is intoxicating. It is powerful.

The more you get, the more you want. Just look at some of the richest, most ruthless men and women throughout history. They had enormous amounts of money —more than they would ever be able to spend in their lifetime- yet it was never enough.

They wanted more. They became addicted to the sense of power and the ability to make as much money as possible.

When you begin to find success with mind control, it will be granting you some incredible powers. Maybe not the ability to take over the world, but certainly the ability to take control of your life.

Many of us feel as though we don't have control of our lives any longer. It's a frustrating sensation and one that can lead us to do some tough things.

When you begin to take control and gain power, you might expand your focus and think that you can help others, especially those about whom you care. You suddenly start to believe that you know what's best for someone else.

Then where do you stop?

Understanding the Power that Mind Control Gives You

Once you begin to see how your mind control strategies work on others, you're going to also recognize the power that it gives you.

Just imagine how incredible it feels to get someone to agree to let you do something, or to have them do something they wouldn't otherwise do.

You feel as though you're a marionette controlling puppets.

You might even start to think to yourself, 'Well, if I can get them to do *that* for me, then what else could I get them to do …'

Suddenly you're tripping down a very dangerous slope. When you begin to expand your mind control power to get others to do anything you want, and everything, then you're no longer in control of yourself.

You've lost touch with reality.

Mind control should only be used for you, to help you. It should be used to get you things that you don't deserve. You shouldn't use mind control to get someone to do your homework for you. That won't help you in the long run.

Be aware of the warning signs that you are beginning to lose control over yourself.

- You're using mind control to get people to help a friend or loved one out.

- You're focused on getting more money for yourself than you need.

- You're exceeding your original goals you set out for mind control.

- You're no longer listening to voices of reason telling you to limit yourself.

- You feel compelled to control others because when you don't, you're feeling empty or hollow.

As with many aspects of life, mind control can be addicting. When you step back and give yourself some time and space, you'll help avoid those challenges as a result.

Don't Abuse It

Drugs are the most common substances that people abuse. People also have a tendency to abuse other people.

Both abuses are rooted in something deep down that we're trying to hide from. Abusive people are usually victims of abuse themselves. They were beaten down or assaulted or had other horrible acts committed against them that they hurt every day. The only way to feel as though they have power in their life, or control, is to abuse others.

Or to abuse alcohol or drugs.

When you don't have high esteem, when you don't think much about yourself, you're going to find that you are more susceptible to abusing drugs or other people.

When you learn how to control others through mind control, you'll also find that it's tempting to want to continue to do more.

I want to end poverty.

I want to change the world.

I want to help people who are homeless get homes.

Most of the horrific crimes throughout history began as seeds of wanting to do something good for the people around them.

Genghis Kahn didn't set out to conquer the world. He set out to push back against the Roman Empire that was invading his people's lands, that were tormenting and killing his people.

King Henry VIII didn't grow up with the intention of destroying millions of lives with war and poverty. He wanted the church to change the rules so he could divorce legally. When they wouldn't, he set out to break away from Vatican law.

Hitler is considered one of the most evil monsters in history. He didn't set out to destroy the world; his focus initially was restoring German superiority and to end the suffering that occurred following World War I.

Not one of history's most vile leaders began with the quest to conquer the world just because they could. They began with intentions of making a difference or of helping someone else.

But then they gained power. Then they won a few minor victories. Soon they became addicted to it.

With mind control, you'll need to be on guard so that you don't get carried away trying to end the struggles of others through the act of controlling others.

If you begin to abuse it, you will find out soon enough that abusing mind control most often ends with the individual losing everything that he or she worked so hard to achieve. At that point, no one will trust you and you will have no more power at all.

Con artists learn this over and over. They simply pack up and move on to a place where no one knows them, and they begin all over again.

Don't abuse your newfound power and you'll be able to hold onto it for a long time.

Chapter 7: Falling for the Media Trap against Mind Control

Why do so many people talk about mind control as though it's some evil thing? Or that only evil people would even think about using it?

First, you need to consider the source. In today's society, 'media' is no longer a dignified profession. Being in media means pursuing a singular agenda, usually that of the founder's or owner's intention.

If you're talking about the news media, then most of it is liberal (or left leaning). Most people would think that has to do with helping the poor, being against the rich and powerful interests, and so on. It's not. It's about control and power.

If you had power, what would you *not* want to encourage in others?

Power.

You would *not* want others to gain power. Nor would you think it was a good idea to encourage people to try and find a way to gain power.

You'd want to make sure that you were the *only* one who had power, and that no one really looked into finding out how to achieve it.

Why So Many Don't Want You to Know about It

Mind control techniques work. It has been proven time and time again throughout history. It's why many people don't want you to know about it.

When you begin slipping in and taking away power from those who have it, that means there's going to be *less* power for them.

Now, if you had become addicted to power (see Chapter 6), you have an insatiable need to acquire more. You also will have a strong desire to keep the power that you have.

It wouldn't matter to you that you got that power through negative acts or by manipulating or deceiving others; as long as you had it, you'd want to keep it all to yourself.

As a result, you wouldn't want anyone else knowing about how to get it. If you begin sharing all of your secrets to gaining power, making tons of money, and more, then you're going to simply be creating more competition for yourself.

So why am I sharing these strategies with you? Why do *I* want you to know about mind control techniques?

Because I'm not greedy. I use mind control to help my career, to get things I want, but I have no ambitions to rule the nation or the world. I have my own little world, friends and family who care about me … what else do I need?

Others, especially the media, politicians, and those with power don't want you to know about mind control. However, it's something that has been talked about in the past, and *proven* to be effective.

How could you keep people away from it then?

Why it's Made Out for be So Evil

The people who are afraid of others learning mind control techniques are those who have something to lose when others gain.

How then do you keep most people away from the information that could free them from their chains? How would you keep people from going after the information that could provide them with so much power?

You make it out to be evil.

You *guilt* people into believing that even the pursuit of such mind control techniques is evil and that when you use them, you're inherently evil.

I hope I showed in the first chapters of this book that *most* mind control techniques are not evil. Not even close.

The abuse of them could be.

It's akin to the gun control debate that rages in this country to this day. The Second Amendment guarantees the right of every citizen to 'keep and bear arms' (guns). However, does the gun kill? Is the gun inherently bad?

Or is it just a tool?

You can debate all you want, but the bottom line is that when a gun is sitting on a table and no touches it, no gets hurt.

If someone breaks into the home and is met by a homeowner with a gun, then it's a protective weapon. It can save that family their possessions and even their lives.

If someone takes that gun out to kill someone with it because they're mad at them, then it's being used for evil.

Mind control is no different. Sitting there idly, it does nothing. It won't harm or help anyone.

Used for positive reasons, it can protect or benefit many people.

Used for negative reasons, it can hurt and damage many people.

It's not evil. If you look behind the curtain of those claiming that mind control *is* evil, you'll see that their true intentions aren't to protect others; it's to protect themselves and to keep what they have.

Why 'They' are all so Wrong

'They' are the people or entities (corporations, for example) that don't want people to learn about mind control.

'They' are wrong when they claim that it's evil because, as described in the previous chapter, mind control is just a tool.

It can be used for good, and it can be used for bad.

'They' are using mind control on you when they claim that it's evil. They are lying … they are *deceiving* you with the intention of keeping you from discovering just what you could do when you master mind control techniques.

You can use mind control to benefit your life.

Or you can use it to hurt others.

What you do with it is entirely up to you, just as the knife in the kitchen could be used to prepare a meal, or to hurt someone.

Don't buy into the hype that it's evil.

Only the person behind the mind control technique will determine if it's used for good or evil purposes.

Chapter 8: Keys to Success with Mind Control

As with anything you do, the keys to being successful lie in a few characteristics. I'll talk about these individually, but simply put, in order to be successful with mind control, you need to:

- Be present

- Use touch

- Make eye contact

- Rely on the power of language

- Interrupt the pattern

Now, let's break each of these down in further detail.

Be present

This one is relatively simple. You need to be present when you're aiming to control someone's mind. That means you need to be focused completely on the topic and the person to whom you're talking.

You can't be thinking about why your favorite sports team lost last night. You can't be worried about 'what if this goes wrong'.

You can't be thinking about the fight you had with your spouse or girlfriend or boyfriend last night.

You need to be completely focused on this moment. The here and now.

Be present. Get your mind focused on what you need to do right now.

Make sure that the person to whom you're talking understands that they are important.

Make sure that they have no doubts about what you're thinking (that you're focused on them).

Be focused on the message you're sending. Be clear.

Use touch

Touch is one of the most intimate things that humans experience. When you touch someone, you're connecting with them on a much deeper level.

Some people don't want to be touched. Other's rely on it.

Know your target and whether he or she is offended by it. If they are, then keep your distance.

The last thing you want is to be accused of sexual harassment because you touched an arm, or placed your hand on a shoulder.

Shake hands. Be firm. Don't go with the light, bent wrist type of handshake. Be confident.

Don't touch someone's leg. Ever. That's never going to be appropriate, even if you're sitting next to that person and they are engaged with you. Unless you've been on at least *one* date with that person, touching the leg is a no-no.

You can lean against them slightly when shoulder to shoulder, such as showing them a graph, chart, or picture. Pat their shoulder when you're leading them somewhere to show them something.

It's that connection, that very personal connection, that can help to remove barriers in their mind.

Make eye contact

A person who lies, or who isn't that confident, will tend to avoid eye contact whenever possible. That's why you should always make eye contact when you can.

The eyes are the gateways to our soul.

Why do you think so many people tell someone, "Look into my eyes and tell me the truth"? It's because it's much harder for people to lie when looking into their eyes. There's something special about the eyes.

The more eye contact you make with your target, the more trusting they will be of you. The more trusting that they are of you, the more likely they will be willing to do what you want, or give you permission to do what you want.

Rely on the power of language

The words you use can make all the difference in the world to getting what you want.

A little boy walks up to his mother and says, *Give me a brownie.*

Is that going to work? Not too often. So what if he walked up to her and said, *Mom, would it be possible for me to have a brownie, please?*

Words make a difference. If you talk to someone and you're cursing and swearing every other word, how can they take you seriously?

There's a misconception being spread throughout social media that people who curse are a lot are more honest.

First, that's not true. Second, people who curse a lot don't have a solid grasp on language, so they rely on the simple, foul language.

It's abrasive. It's course. It's rude.

If you want to be effective with mind control, be aware of your language. The right words can shape opinion.

Use active verbs instead of passive. i.e. This *will* improve your company's bottom line … is far more active and confident than 'This could have a positive impact on your bottom line.'

Be succinct whenever possible.

As the sun's light penetrates the ozone layer of the earth, the prism effect of light creates the illusion that the sky is actually blue.

Huh? What?

No. How about *The sky is blue.*

Don't try and muddy the waters by using tricky words no one could possibly understand.

The cantankerous curmudgeon was called a troglodyte by his spouse before she turned on her voluptuous heels and clomped out the front door.

First, people are going to ask you what half those words mean. That gets them off guard.

Second, you could say that simpler. *She called her mean, nasty husband a cave troll before she stormed out the door.*

Language will tell a lot about a person. Make sure yours sends the right message.

Interrupt the pattern

When you listen to good poetry, or exceptional music, there's a rhythm to it that not only enhances the message (words) but that can also hit your emotional triggers.

When you're making a speech, you don't drone on in a monotone voice because people would fall asleep too quickly.

Alter the pattern and the rhythm. The minute that your target starts to get comfortable with the rhythm, the moment they begin to see a pattern, that's the moment they begin putting their guard up.

Mind control works when you bring people's guard down.

When you rehearse your approach, look for a pattern. Any pattern (there's usually one there). Once you find it, break it.

Interrupt the pattern and you continue to control the message and that's what you want.

Chapter 9: 5 Simple Rules to Follow

In order to make mind control work for you, and to be successful with it, there are a few rules that you should keep in mind.

You can certainly ignore any or all of them, but if you do, you decrease the chances that you'll actually be successful.

These 5 simple rules are:

- Create a win-win situation
- Be present
- Make up their mind *for* them
- Be consistent
- Reframe it if there is no benefit

Now, let's look at these more closely. One of them should look familiar, because it is. But it's that important.

Create a win-win situation

While you want a situation in which *you* gain something, the more of a win-win that you can create, the more impressive it will be for you and your target.

How do you create a win-win situation? Essentially you need to know what the person would want out of any deal or relationship.

That's when you need to do your research first and foremost.

The job that you can't wait to get: what does the employer *really* need? They may state that they're looking for the generic things like honesty and integrity, but what about the person who is a born leader? What about the young man or woman who is willing to put in extra hours, who isn't looking to cash in on every single minute, but is looking for the career opportunity? What about the employee who would be treating this business like his or her own?

The child growing up who wants to get a car would need to know what his parents would want in that car. Safety would be feature number one. While the kid probably wants a slick, powerful beast, sticking with the highest safety rated cars would be giving the parent their win in the situation.

The more you know about what the target wants, the more you'll be able to build those win-win situations.

Those are hard to turn down, and you effectively control the mind at that point.

Be present

As stated in the previous chapter, you really need to be there, in the moment, completely and totally focused on the person to whom you're talking.

If you're talking to someone who is distracted, who asks you to hold on while they read and reply to a text, or who constantly has to silence their phone, then what happens?

You become annoyed first. Second, you lose interest.

The moment someone loses interest in what you're saying is the moment that you begin to lose him or her.

Mind control only works when they are interested in what you have to say. And in order to get that, you need to be present, in the moment, completely and totally focused on them.

Make up their mind *for* them

When you begin to look around and notice some characteristics of people everywhere, you'll notice that most of them want to have other people make decisions for them.

They hem and haw. They're wishy-washy. They simply don't *want* to have to make their mind up.

Maybe that's all they do every single day at work: make decisions.

Maybe they just don't trust their own judgment.

They are actively looking for someone to help them make up their mind for them.

Once you make their mind up for them, you need to move to the close and get them to commit.

Yes, *when* you hire me, it's going to be the best decision you can make.

If you let me get this car, you're going to know that I'll be safe driving.

When you agree to a date with me, you'll know you're going to have a great time.

People are always looking for those who will make decisions. When you step up and do that, you're going to find that controlling the rest of the situation to be that much easier to do.

Be consistent

You absolutely *must* be consistent. The entire time that you're working on manipulating, deceiving, or persuading someone about something, you need to be consistent.

When you're not, you will create massive holes that you would then need to navigate around.

It's easy to get caught in a lie, which is what makes deception so tough. You need to keep in mind that all of the small lies that you may tell or the things that you do in order to deceive need to be kept in order.

The moment that you slip and say something that doesn't align with something else you said, you're going to have problems.

People want to trust people. If you're not consistent, then you're not really all that trustworthy to begin with.

Focus on being consistent. You'll also find that the longer it takes for you to control someone else's mind, thoughts, and decisions, the tougher it's going to be to remain consistent, but you need to be. From start to finish.

Reframe it if there is no benefit

If there is no apparent benefit for the target, then you need to reframe your focal point. After all, we live in a simple world: *what's in it for me?*

A parent is not going to give their kid the hotrod sports car unless there's something in it for them. Usually, it's buying affection, which never works in the long run, anyway.

However, focusing on a practical, safe car will give them some peace of mind.

The employer looking to hire a new manager wants someone who will take charge, be trustworthy, and who they can leave in charge from time to time.

If your manipulation, persuasion, or deception technique isn't going to offer any real benefit to the target, then you need to reframe your approach. That doesn't mean you won't be able to control their mind; it means that it will be that much tougher for you to do it, unless you frame it

all so that they see the benefit that it could offer.

Conclusion: Mind Control Begins ...

Mind control begins, essentially, within your mind. If you don't have a strong mind, if you don't have confidence in yourself, then your challenge is going to be that much greater to control someone else.

Forget the notion of guilt that you may be feeling. If you're not going to hurt anyone, if you're going to improve your position in life without diminishing someone else's, then you have nothing to feel guilty about when you start controlling their mind.

It's a matter of confidence that should be your primary starting point.

In order to be confident, you need to understand your hopes, dreams, and ambitions. Once you do, you'll be in a better position to control the conversation and that will help you strengthen your mind control techniques.

Anyone can control other's thoughts and feelings. We do it all the time without thinking about it.

Once you become more conscious about it, you'll be able to refine your focus and go after things more actively, rather than passively.

Once you begin down this path, you'll find doors opening to you that you never thought were possible.

Now, let the mind control begin …